PARALLEL LIVES

HILLARY CLINTON
Born in 1947
TEMPLE GRANDIN

Julie Knutson

Published in the United States of America by Cherry Lake Publishing
Ann Arbor, Michigan
www.cherrylakepublishing.com

Reading Adviser: Marla Conn, MS, Ed., Literacy specialist, Read-Ability, Inc.
Cover Designer: Felicia Macheske

Photo Credits: © Library of Congress/Maureen Keating, photographer, 1993./www.loc.gov/item/2017650165/, cover, 1 [left]; © Rosalie Winard, cover, 2 [right]; © Library of Congress, LC-USF346-024216-D, 5; © PatrickGorski/iStock.com, 6; © Joe Tabb/Dreamstime.com, 9; © Alan C. Heison/Shutterstock.com, 10; © PeopleImages/iStock.com, 12; © Sergio Torres Baus/Dreamstime.com, 15; © Gregory Reed/Shutterstock.com, 16; © bamby-bhamby/iStock.com, 19; © Galina Niederhaus/Shutterstock.com, 21; © Grant Heilman Photography/Alamy Stock Photo, 22; © becon/iStock.com, 24; © andresr/iStock.com, 25; © Kathy Hutchins/Shutterstock.com, 26

Copyright ©2020 by Cherry Lake Publishing
All rights reserved. No part of this book may be reproduced or utilized in any form or by any means without written permission from the publisher.

Library of Congress Cataloging-in-Publication Data

Names: Knutson, Julie, author.
Title: Born in 1947 : Hillary Clinton and Temple Grandin / by Julie Knutson.
Description: Ann Abor, Michigan : Cherry Lake Publishing, [2020]. | Series: Parallel lives | Includes bibliographical references and index. | Audience: Grades 4-6
Identifiers: LCCN 2019033472 | ISBN 9781534159211 (hardcover) | ISBN 9781534161511 (paperback) | ISBN 9781534160361 (pdf) | ISBN 9781534162662 (ebook)
Subjects: LCSH: Clinton, Hillary Rodham—Juvenile literature. | Grandin, Temple—Juvenile literature. | Presidents' spouses—United States—Biography—Juvenile literature. | Women cabinet officers—United States—Biography—Juvenile literature. | Cabinet officers—United States—Biography—Juvenile literature. | Women legislators—United States—Biography—Juvenile literature. | Legislators—United States—Biography—Juvenile literature. | Women presidential candidates—United States—Biography—Juvenile literature. | Presidential candidates—United States—Biography—Juvenile literature. | Autistic people—United States—Biography—Juvenile literature. | Animal scientists—United States—Biography—Juvenile literature. | Women animal specialists—United States—Biography—Juvenile literature. | Animal specialists—United States—Biography—Juvenile literature. | Animal welfare—United States—Juvenile literature.
Classification: LCC E887.C55 K58 2020 | DDC 973.932092 [B]—dc23
LC record available at https://lccn.loc.gov/2019033472

Cherry Lake Publishing would like to acknowledge the work of the Partnership for 21st Century Learning, a Network of Battelle for Kids. Please visit www.battelleforkids.org/networks/p21 for more information.

Printed in the United States of America
Corporate Graphics

ABOUT THE AUTHOR

Julie Knutson shares a birth year with Venus Williams, Chelsea Clinton, and Lin-Manuel Miranda. An avid student of history and former teacher, she lives in northern Illinois with her husband and son.

TABLE OF CONTENTS

CHAPTER 1
Welcome to 1947 4

CHAPTER 2
Hillary Clinton (b. October 26, 1947) 8

CHAPTER 3
Temple Grandin (b. August 29, 1947) 18

TIMELINE 28-29
RESEARCH AND ACT 30
FURTHER READING 30
GLOSSARY 31
INDEX 32

CHAPTER 1

Welcome to 1947

1947. Politician Hillary Clinton and animal welfare pioneer Temple Grandin are born 2 years after World War II has ended. The United States and Soviet Union are engaged in a new conflict: the **Cold War**, a decades-long period of global tension. For some Americans, this era spelled new wealth and higher standards of living. **Suburbs** linked by networks of highways cropped up. Advertisements showed happy families whose lives were made easier by dazzling machines and packaged foods. Hillary and Temple were shaped by the social forces that swirled around them. Other notable developments of the late 1940s and 1950s influenced their lives and careers.

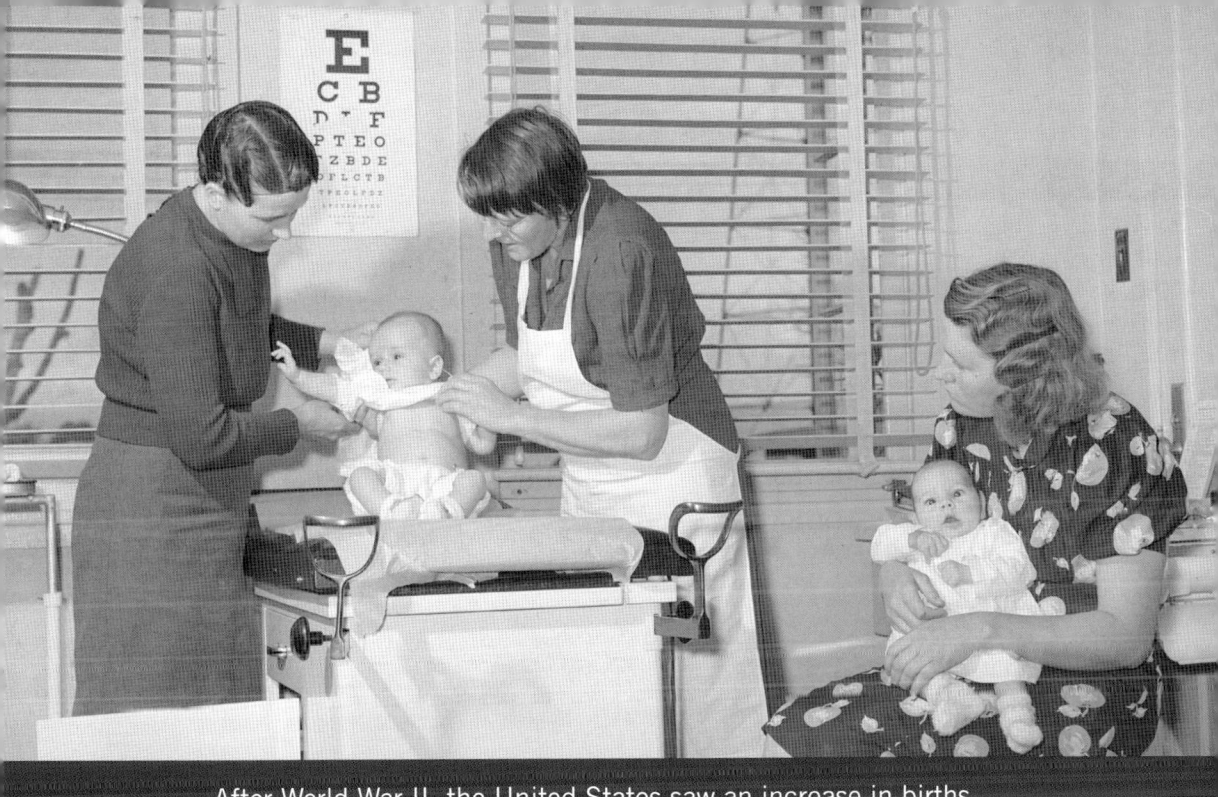

After World War II, the United States saw an increase in births. Babies born between 1946 and 1964 are considered "baby boomers."

Gender: In magazines and on television, women were often presented as happy homemakers. They wore perfect dresses and turned out piping-hot meals for their hungry, smiling families. The reality for many women—particularly women of color—was quite different. But this **norm** was widely accepted, and heavily influenced perceptions of women. Career options for women were limited, and throughout the 1950s, leadership roles were dominated by men.

The McDonald brothers opened up a restaurant selling 15-cent hamburgers in 1948. They would later turn this model into the chain McDonald's we know today.

Agricultural Shifts: Fast food became a part of the American diet in the 1940s. The trend of cheap, convenient food continued into the following decades. Restaurants wanted burgers and fries that tasted the same in all their **chain stores**, whether in Illinois or Idaho. The agriculture industry responded by making more **specialized** farms. In order to produce products that were exactly alike, these farms focused on just one type of food. Many **livestock** producers began to house massive herds of cows, pigs, or chickens. Their operations turned farms into factories, emphasizing efficiency and convenience over compassion for animals.

The Cold War

*The Cold War lasted from the mid-1940s through the early 1990s. During this period, the United States and Soviet Union had competing visions of how best to govern. Each sought to spread their ideas worldwide through threats and **propaganda**. With both powers holding nuclear weapons, many feared atomic warfare.*

CHAPTER 2

Hillary Clinton
(b. October 26, 1947)

Hillary Rodham Clinton is a woman of many "firsts." In the 1970s, she was the first female lawyer hired by an all-male law firm in its 156-year history. She was New York's first woman senator. She was the first (and, so far, only) former First Lady to serve as secretary of state. And in 2016, she was the first woman nominated by a major political party for U.S. president. In all of these roles, she used her voice to present solutions to pressing issues like health care, education, and international relations. She also supports equal opportunities for women and girls.

Hillary campaigned under the slogan "I'm With Her."

In 1983, Sally Ride became the first female astronaut in space for the United States.

Early Years: Finding a Voice

Hillary was born on October 26, 1947, and grew up in the suburbs of Chicago, Illinois. She had two brothers, but her parents didn't treat her differently because she was a girl. Instead, they told her that if she worked hard, she could achieve anything. Her parents and community stressed other messages that shaped her growth. At home and at church, she heard, "Do the most good that you can." Her mother also emphasized that she should "never back down from a bully." Throughout her childhood and into her career, she never did.

Drawing on the idea of "doing the most good," young Hillary tried to solve problems in her community and beyond it. When she learned about the struggles of migrant farmworkers, she babysat for their children and planned a backyard game fundraiser. She believed in the power of talking to and learning from peers of all backgrounds. Through her youth group, she met African American and Latino kids in Chicago. She experienced the power of face-to-face conversation in breaking down walls.

Hillary developed her voice throughout high school and college. As a senior at Wellesley College, she was selected to give the first

A letter to NASA

In 1961, Hillary Clinton wrote a letter to the National Aeronautics and Space Administration (NASA) asking how she could become an astronaut. The agency wrote back stating that women weren't candidates for space travel. Hillary remembered the feeling that letter gave her: "It was the first time I had hit an obstacle I couldn't overcome with hard work and determination, and I was outraged." She vowed to never let anyone or anything stop her from achieving her dreams, just because of her gender.

[BORN IN 1947: HILLARY CLINTON AND TEMPLE GRANDIN]

At Yale Law School, Hillary was one of 27 women in a class of 235.

student graduation speech in the school's history. She spoke following a senator who discouraged the students from protesting. Hillary countered this view, telling her fellow graduates, "The challenge now is to practice politics as the art of making what appears to be impossible, possible." Seven minutes of applause followed her speech, which was profiled in *LIFE* magazine.

Middle Years: Expressing a Voice

Following graduation, Hillary set off for Yale Law School in Connecticut. Social justice was central to her pursuits. In the summers, she worked to get migrant children in Florida access to health care and schooling. She also helped **mobilize** minority voters in Texas and advocated for children's rights through the Children's Defense Fund.

Hillary met Bill Clinton at law school. The pair fell in love and moved to Bill's home state of Arkansas. There he began his political career. Hillary taught law, managed a successful business practice, served as Arkansas's First Lady, and gave birth to their daughter, Chelsea. In 1992, Bill was elected president of the United States.

Throughout Bill's presidency, Hillary was often criticized for being too **outspoken**, involved, and **opinionated**. But she wasn't going to sit by and do nothing. Bill appointed her to create a plan to provide health care to all Americans. The plan was defeated, but Hillary didn't let that push her out of the public eye. She traveled internationally, using her position to pressure governments to uphold human rights for women and girls.

After her time in the White House, Hillary pursued political ambitions of her own. She wanted to continue to do the most good. In 2000, she was elected as a senator from New York. In 2008, she made her first bid for president, running in the Democratic primaries against Barack Obama. She lost the tight race but was appointed secretary of state after Obama became president.

Making Headlines

Hillary Clinton gave a speech at a 1995 United Nations summit in China. She said, "Women's rights are human rights, once and for all." The Chinese government banned the media from printing Hillary's statement. But the strength and passion with which she delivered it made headlines around the world.

Hillary was a senator for New York during the September 11 attacks. She defended the rights of victims and families.

Hillary received about 2.8 million more votes than Donald Trump in the 2016 presidential election. In U.S. history, this is the largest margin to result in a loss.

She served in that role from 2009 to 2013, during which time she traveled to 112 countries, more than any who had served before her. She advocated for a "smart power" strategy. This meant that the United States avoided military force. Instead, it worked to build international relations through **diplomacy** and economic development. Her time as secretary of state was also marked by attention to climate change and women's issues.

Later Years: Leaving a Legacy

In 2016, Hillary again ran for president. This time, she won the Democratic Party's nomination. Her opponent was Donald Trump. Her campaign emphasized issues such as women's rights, child care, and access to equal pay for equal work. She held a steady lead in polls until 11 days before the election. That was when the FBI reopened an investigation into her use of a private email server during her time as secretary of state. While she won the **popular vote**, she lost the **electoral college**. She was later cleared of any wrongdoing.

In Hillary's **concession** speech, she said, "To all the little girls watching this, never doubt that you are valuable and powerful and deserving of every chance and opportunity in the world to pursue and achieve your own dreams." Staying true to her voice, she continues to write, speak, and work on behalf of the causes that drove her career. Her impact is also seen in the growing number of women serving in public office. In 2018, more women were elected to Congress than ever before.

CHAPTER 3

Temple Grandin
(b. August 29, 1947)

"I like the way I think," says Temple Grandin. "It's the ultimate virtual reality (VR) system." Throughout her life and career, Temple has used her ability to think in pictures. Her inner VR system helps her to **empathize** with animals and design more humane practices for the treatment of livestock. She has overcome labels, judgment, and crippling anxiety to do this work. Today, she serves as an ambassador within and beyond the **autism** community. She preaches the importance of following your passions to create meaningful change in the world.

Temple is famous for saying, "I am different, not less."

Early Years: Finding a Voice

Temple Grandin was born on August 29, 1947, in Boston, Massachusetts. She didn't speak until she was 3 years old. She hated being hugged and avoided looking people in the eye. Sounds and smells overwhelmed her. She had no verbal way of letting her parents know these things upset her, so she communicated through screams and fits. She drew on walls and chewed puzzle pieces. Temple's parents were concerned.

Temple's mother took the 3-year-old to the doctor in Boston. The doctor said Temple had autism. Her father thought she should be sent away to a place doctors could look after her. But her mother felt differently and decided to try to build her daughter's speech and social skills. With help from tutors, teachers, family, and peers, Temple became better able to cope with the world around her.

Temple loved animals and enjoyed physical work. It distracted her from her anxiety. This led her mother to send her to her aunt's ranch during summer break. While there, Temple studied the cows.

Autism Spectrum Disorders

As of 2018, autism spectrum disorders (ASDs) affected 1 in 59 American children. One of the key features of autism is difficulty with communication and social interaction. The symptoms and severity of the disorder vary widely. Teaching language and social skills early greatly benefits people with ASDs.

Some people with ASDs, including Temple Grandin, struggle with language. Temple thinks in pictures rather than words. As her work shows, this isn't a "disadvantage." **Neurodiversity** *is the idea that the world needs and benefits from all types of minds. Temple's life and work have advanced this important concept.*

Cows are sensitive and playful. Some people use them for emotional support or therapy.

Inspired by the cattle squeeze, Temple's device is often called a hug machine.

She observed how they reacted to loud sounds. She saw their nerves at being unexpectedly touched and how they jumped at the sudden sight of objects. Temple realized that cows understood her and that she understood them.

One day, a veterinarian came to vaccinate the herd. The cows were nervous, twitching and mooing to express their fear. But then they were guided into a squeeze chute, a machine that used gentle pressure to make the cows stand still. This calmed and quieted them. Temple put the pieces together. She experienced the world as many animals do. If this machine could calm them, could it calm her too?

She convinced her aunt to let her try the machine. It worked! It gave Temple the comfort of a hug that she'd always wanted but had never been able to tolerate physically. She was flooded with peace and relief. She wanted a squeeze machine of her own. When she returned to school, she built a **prototype**. She tested it on peers and recorded the results. Temple the scientist identified a problem, found a solution, and made it a reality.

People for the Ethical Treatment of Animals (PETA) was formed in 1980.

Middle Years: Expressing a Voice

Temple went on to college and then graduate school. After that, she wanted to apply her unique viewpoint and design skills to make life better for cattle. She redesigned beef processing plants to make them kinder and more efficient. However, in the 1970s, the world of livestock was largely closed to women. Temple managed to get in through writing. She presented her pioneering ideas in industry magazines. She wrote that healthy, happy cattle—free from pain and fear—produced better products. She discouraged the use of

According to studies at the University of Wisconsin-Madison, happy cows make better milk.

Temple's life was made into an HBO film. It won many awards.

force. And she said facilities should be designed for animal comfort, not just human convenience. Ranchers and cattlemen started paying attention.

Temple sought to translate the experiences of voiceless animals. While some people were open to her ideas, others were not. Temple endured verbal abuse and physical threats. Her car was once smeared with animal blood and organs. Nevertheless, she created countless devices and strategies—from a "dipping vat" for herds with **mites** to a survey for measuring cow distress. These are now standard in the industry today.

Later Years: Leaving a Legacy

Temple Grandin proved that "different" isn't "less." Through books and public appearances, she provides hope to people with ASDs and their families. She has shown that, if their interests are encouraged, children who don't fit the norm can do incredible things. Temple has used her voice to speak up for animals and to express that the world needs all kinds of minds. In the process, she has forever changed how animals are treated and how people think about autism.

Meat Consumption in the United States

In 2018, the average American ate 222.2 pounds (100.8 kilograms) of meat (including beef, poultry, and pork). This was a record high.

TIMELINE

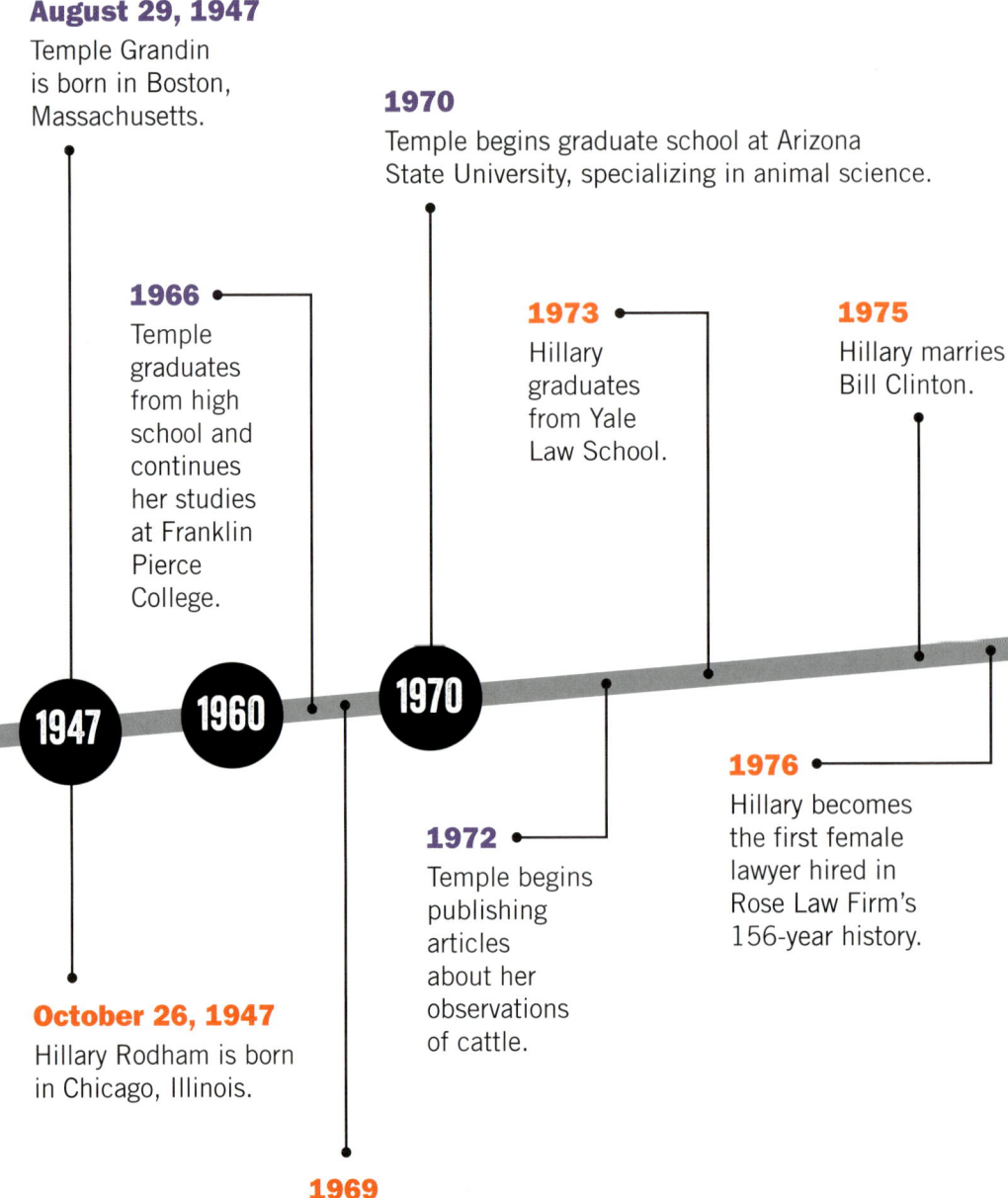

August 29, 1947
Temple Grandin is born in Boston, Massachusetts.

1966
Temple graduates from high school and continues her studies at Franklin Pierce College.

1970
Temple begins graduate school at Arizona State University, specializing in animal science.

1973
Hillary graduates from Yale Law School.

1975
Hillary marries Bill Clinton.

1972
Temple begins publishing articles about her observations of cattle.

1976
Hillary becomes the first female lawyer hired in Rose Law Firm's 156-year history.

October 26, 1947
Hillary Rodham is born in Chicago, Illinois.

1969
Hillary graduates from Wellesley College, delivering the first student graduation speech in the school's history.

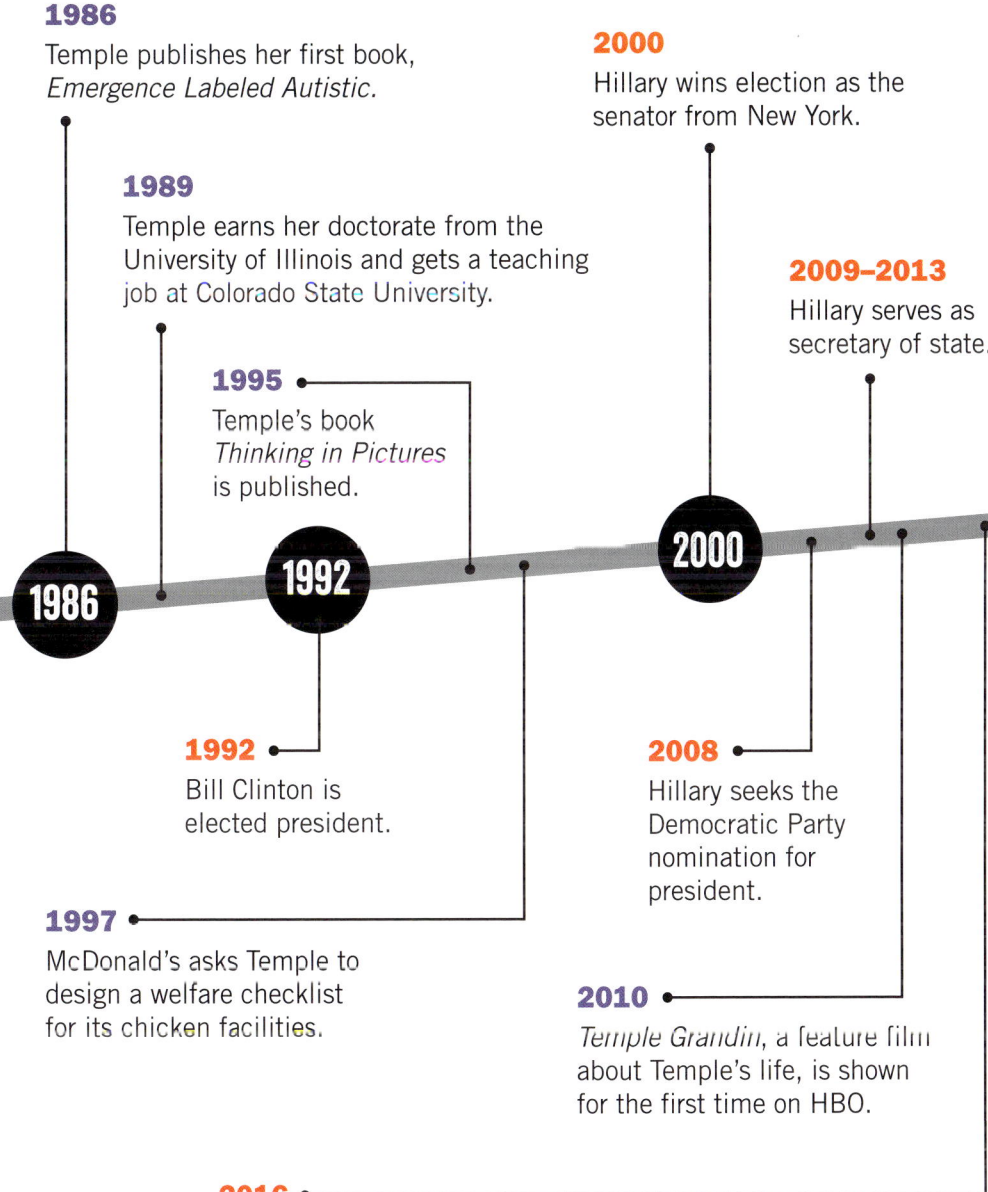

[BORN IN 1947: HILLARY CLINTON AND TEMPLE GRANDIN]

Research and Act

Hillary Clinton and Temple Grandin are both problem solvers who have devoted their careers to finding solutions for different issues and challenges.

Research
Research problems facing your community. You might want to focus on hunger, homelessness, or the environment. What organizations are addressing these challenges, and how?

Act
Be a part of the solution to the cause you chose! Reach out to community organizations to learn how you can help. Use your voice to educate peers on the subject. Invite guest speakers to your class, volunteer, or hold a fundraiser.

Further Reading

Alexander, Heather. *Who Is Hillary Clinton?* New York, NY: Grosset & Dunlap, 2016.

Guglielmo, Amy. *How to Build a Hug: Temple Grandin and Her Amazing Squeeze Machine.* New York, NY: Atheneum Books for Young Readers, 2018.

Loh-Hagan, Virginia. *Temple Grandin and Livestock Handling.* Ann Arbor, MI: Cherry Lake Publishing, 2018.

Markel, Michelle. *Hillary Rodham Clinton: Some Girls Are Born to Lead.* New York, NY: Balzer + Bray, 2016.

Montgomery, Sy. *Temple Grandin: How the Girl Who Loved Cows Embraced Autism and Changed the World.* Boston, MA: Houghton Mifflin Harcourt, 2012.

Ventura, Marne. *Hillary Clinton: Historic Politician.* Minneapolis, MN: Core Library, 2018.

GLOSSARY

autism (AW-tiz-uhm) disorder marked by difficulty with communication and social skills

chain stores (CHAYN STORZ) a group of stores or restaurants owned by the same company and selling similar products

Cold War (KOHLD WOR) 45-year period of tense rivalry between the United States and Soviet Union

concession (kuhn-SESH-uhn) admitting defeat in an election

diplomacy (dih-PLOH-muh-see) maintaining international relations, often through negotiation and treaties

electoral college (ih-LEK-tor-uhl KAH-lij) a group of electors from each state in the country that together determines who becomes president

empathize (EM-puh-thize) to understand another's feelings

livestock (LIVE-stahk) farm animals

mites (MITES) tiny animals with eight legs that are like spiders and mostly live on plants and animals

mobilize (MOH-buh-lize) push to action

neurodiversity (noor-oh-dih-VUR-sih-tee) variety in brain structure and mental function

norm (NORM) socially expected standard

opinionated (uh-PIN-yuh-nate-id) holding strongly to one's own opinion about something

outspoken (out-SPOH-kuhn) very honest and direct, especially when criticizing someone or something

popular vote (PAHP-yuh-lur VOHT) total number of votes in a U.S. election

propaganda (prah-puh-GAN-duh) information designed to promote a particular political view or cause

prototype (PROH-tuh-tipe) the first version of an invention that tests an idea to see if it will work

specialized (SPESH-uh-lized) focused on the production of one item

suburbs (SUHB-urbz) outlying areas that surround a city

INDEX

agriculture, 7
animal welfare, 4, 18–27
autism spectrum disorders, 18, 20, 27

baby boomers, 5

cattle. *See* cows; livestock
Clinton, Bill, 13
Clinton, Hillary Rodham, 4, 8–17
   early years, 10–13
   education, 11–13
   as first lady, 14
   "firsts," 8
   legacy, 17
   middle years, 13–16
   as politician, 14–16
   runs for president, 16–17
   as Secretary of State, 14, 16
Cold War, 4, 7
communication, 20
cows, 20–23. *See also* livestock

diplomacy, 16

education, 11–13, 24
empathy, 18
equal opportunities, 8

farming, 7
fast food, 7
food production, 7

gender, 5
Grandin, Temple, 4, 18–27
   designs products for livestock comfort, 24–26
   early years, 19–23
   education, 24
   legacy, 27
   middle years, 24–26

health care, 14
hug machine, 22
human rights, 14

livestock, 7, 18, 24. *See also* cows

McDonald's, 6

NASA, 11
neurodiversity, 20

People for the Ethical Treatment of Animals (PETA), 24
politics, 4, 8–17

Ride, Sally, 10

social interaction, 20
social justice, 13
squeeze chute, 22, 23
suburbs, 4

timeline, 28–29
Trump, Donald, 16, 17

women
after World War II, 5